Life TO THE
Limits

Life TO THE Limits

From Everyday Losses to New Possibilities

RÉMI PARENT

Translated by Peter Heinegg

LIGUORI/TRIUMPH
LIGUORI, MISSOURI

Published by Liguori/Triumph
An Imprint of Liguori Publications
Liguori, Missouri

Published in 1998 by special arrangement with Paulines, Montreal, Quebec.

Original edition *La vie, un corps à corps avec la mort*
Copyright 1996 Paulines

English translation Copyright 1998 by Liguori Publications

Library of Congress Cataloging-in-Publication Data

Parent, Rémi, 1936–
    [Vie. English]
    Life to the limits : from everyday losses to new possibilities / Rémi Parent : translated by Peter Heinegg — 1st ed.
       p.   cm.
    Includes bibliographical references.
    ISBN 0-7648-0185-6
    1. Christian life—Catholic authors. 2. Loss (Psychology)— Religious aspects—Catholic Church. 3. Death—Religious aspects—Catholic Church. I. Title.
BX2350.2.P32213   1998
248.8'6—dc21   97–53211

Printed in the United States of America
02 01 00 99 98   5 4 3 2 1
First U.S. Edition

Contents

Introduction

There is no hope beyond the grave that doesn't plunge its roots into the depths of the abyss. The credibility of any religious answer to the question of life depends on its capacity literally to open up the tombs. Only those who have the courage to "descend into hell" can talk about "heaven" and in that way try to snatch a whole life from the captivity of death.[1]

*W*hen we welcome the offer of salvation by Jesus Christ, that opens up a place for hope in our human lives. Jesus Christ has become the Living One, henceforth capable of opening the tombs, all the tombs, and snatching our whole existence from the captivity of death. No abyss is deep enough to stifle within it our loveliest desires—desires for life, desires for love, freedom, and justice.

The victory of Jesus Christ over death, however, has nothing in common with some sort of magical intervention that, outside and independent of death, would serve to cure our problems with life and to calm our anxieties. Nor does the liberating dynamism of faith have anything in common with the optimism of consoling discourses—even when the consoler swathes himself in the mantle of a deity. No hope for something beyond the grave and no response to the questions of life can be credible without the courage of a descent into hell. Jesus, a free man, had the courage to make such a descent, the courage to plunge into the depths of the abyss. That is why our faith can become hope, a word of hope uttered from the hollow of the tombs, and strong enough, we believe, to open them.

∞

For some ten years I have very much wanted to write a book about death. Still, I have to admit that once I started on this work, my head and hands began to hesitate and occasionally feel paralyzed. Why these hesitations and this paralysis? I am gauging more carefully just how hard the task is and how crucial in its implications.

Death: The word itself is enough to frighten us, so strongly does it evoke a reality we spontaneously perceive as the very opposite of life. Death doesn't have the appeal of smooth, rounded forms. It hurts us when it visits our existence. Why devote a book to it and invite readers to take the time for a reflective meditation on it? Why waste time in the presence of that undesirable companion?

Death, as I shall try to show throughout the length of our journey together, must not be located exclusively in the last moment of our existence, the one that will mean the end of our life. Death marks our whole existence, all our days, all our activities. And I am sure that there's an indispensable key here to understanding the meaning of life, whether personal or collective—provided that one wishes to live in a way worthy of the human beings that we are.

First of all, let's acknowledge the fact: One has to have lived a little to know that our existence is not a pure welling up of life. Death is always at work in it. Sometimes it takes the form of a sick body that comes to kill projects we were attached to; or the gap that yawns between young people and adults and that, even within families, brings death to so many dreams; or some love or another that we thought would be stronger than everything but that slowly runs out of steam; or an unbearable distribution of wealth that fails to assure the survival of certain persons or even of certain nations; or the countless firings that nowadays condemn so many people to insecurity and shatter personal and family existence; or in some of our societies the frightening rate of teenage suicide (what is the unhappiness with life that makes death more attractive, or less intolerable, than the decision to live?).

So our everyday life is at stake here. Depending on the emphasis we give to death as we live it daily, our existence either enters upon a path of liberation or progressively drifts into alienation.

It does no good to try every means to shirk the challenges we face. Is it possible to live freely and humanly when we haven't incorporated the burden of death? The stakes are high. And if we want to learn about life, keeping our eyes shut tight and thinking we can ignore the constant coming of death are the wrong way to do it. To the extent that we ignore the omnipresence of death, we play into its hands: Instead of making life, we risk sowing death in us and all around us.

∞

Once we have our attention drawn to everyday life, here is how I would describe the conviction that fills every page of this book: *A spirituality, any spirituality at all, isn't worthy of a human being if it doesn't take death seriously, if it doesn't integrate it as an active element of all human existence.* For his part, Jesus Christ doesn't put off the opening of the tomb until the end of time. As the Good News never ceases proclaiming, "Today is the day of salvation!" Thus it is today that Jesus Christ wants to snatch our life from the captivity of death. What sort of disciples would we be if we paid no attention to the present moment and to the challenges death is already throwing in its face? To what hope are we the witnesses when we talk about everyday life and pass death over in silence, the burden of death that we live out every day?

Like it or not, death is always there. Always there...

wherever there is life. I can leave it in anonymity, believing that in this way I can devote better energies to the service of life. But such negligence or fear in the presence of death only gives it free access. Death dictates its laws and, the more we avoid looking the unnamed and unnameable phantom in the eye, manipulates our lives.

"I hope there'll be hope in it," said someone who heard that I was writing this book. One thing I am certain of: We are wretched artificers of hope if we don't bear witness to Jesus Christ from the pit of our deaths, if we don't rise up and march forth from the pit of our captivity. And how can we learn compassion for others, let ourselves be touched by their suffering and pain, accompany them on a path that we want—both they and I—to be a path of life, if we are incapable of living our deaths and of taking on, as freely as possible, our own individual grief?

⟬∾⟭

In an earlier book I tried to express the revolutionary power of Christian faith.[2] In so doing I focused on my own personal approach. My book insisted on a wager that I believe is still possible: The Easter event of Jesus Christ allows us to enter a life that can already, here and now, conquer death.

My book, I hope, told the truth. Still, it made no claim to have said *everything* about Christian life. That life is too complex and too rich to be covered from a single viewpoint. Furthermore, the book, from its first pages and despite its explicit intention to insist on life, had to take into consideration the burden of limits and suffering that is the lot of every human existence and hence of the human existence of Christian believers.

All of us desire to achieve the simple life that has at last become perfectly unified. But everyone knows that there is a world of difference between "simple" and "simplistic." Our longing for simplicity has never had the right to veer off into simplism. And it *would* be simplistic to imagine a Christian existence forever installed in a permanent "alleluia," an unconstrained gushing forth, an unquenchable overflowing of a life now free from all limits and no longer needing to confront death. That sort of spirituality would provide a cheap brand of enthusiasm and consolation. But I don't think it would be worthy of the meaning that Jesus Christ proposes for the women and men of our world.

My next book, provisionally titled *Easter, All Easter,* will attempt to see how Christian faith invites us to reconcile the two points of view (*life/death*) in the unity of one and the same existence. But this sort of reconciliation demands, first of all, that the place of death in our existence be more clearly articulated. That is the objective that we shall pursue now. It is a limited objective, but still an essential one if we wish to be persons and communities that, from a Christian standpoint, are alive.

The formula used may seem abrupt, even brutal: *Nobody can decide to live without deciding to die.* So we shall be talking about death out of fidelity to Jesus Christ, but also out of fidelity to ourselves and out of love for those whom we welcome as brothers and sisters in humanity and for whom, just as for us, *there is never any living without dying.*

Life TO THE Limits

Part One

The Difficult Decision
to Live

*T*he Christian faith, as my earlier book said, confesses a love that opens in our lives a perfectly cleared-away horizon: Thanks to Jesus Christ, each one of us can live a full love of himself or herself, of others, and of God. Such a confession links up with and gives life to a whole part of ourselves, perhaps the loveliest part, which is the field of our desires. The impossible has finally become possible.

But the question inevitably arises: Where is death awaiting us, if everything has been accomplished and if no dike could hold back the conquering flood of Christian love? Isn't it overdramatizing to speak of life as a grappling with death, of a struggle against the everyday world?

And yet, despite the life that we confess, there are moments in our existence that are spread over by a heavy odor of death. Just recently, within the space of two days, a friend of mine learned that a metastasized cancer would be leaving him only a few months with his wife and children; I received a letter attesting to my permanent disability; and a neighbor, the father of two young children, lost his job. At the same time, the TV news was bringing us closer to nations torn by fratricidal war; it almost made us citizens of countries torn apart by death. It is especially on days like these that an irresistible question arises: Isn't the accomplishment of love just an unattainable ideal? Is faith anything more than an empty dream?

The gospel is far from consigning Christians to a sort

of passive enjoyment of salvation. It doesn't promise them a beatific, immobile satisfaction. Anyone who says yes to salvation can no longer be content with being a voyeur of life, a spectator watching the procession of the living as it passes. And it's precisely for this reason that faith, the life of faith, cannot itself escape from daily death.

1

The Experience of Limits

In the Gospel according to Luke (6:47–49) Jesus says: "Everyone who comes to me and hears my words *and does them*, I will tell you what he is like: he is like a man building a house, who dug deeply and laid the foundation on rock." No torrent, no flood can shake that house, because it has been "well built." On the other hand, "the one who hears *and does act*" is like a man who has built his house "on the ground without a foundation," against which the stream broke, and "immediately it fell, and great was the ruin of that house."

The two men hear the same words of Jesus. So what sets them apart and judges them is not mere listening. It's the "putting into practice." No one can be content with hearing the Good News of salvation. It is still strictly necessary to put it into practice. Behaving each day of our lives like the sons and daughters of God, brothers and sisters, with hearts open wide—*that* is what lays the foundation of our life of faith upon rock. Without action, we are doomed to collapse to a "great ruin."

The situation is complicated by the fact that there is and can be no putting anything into practice without a *decision* on our part. Neither God, nor Jesus Christ, nor the angels, nor the authorities, even the religious ones, no one can make our decisions for us. "Here and now"— that is, *where* we exist and *in the today* of our history— we have to decide to live, or not, according to what we profess. Then life undertakes to teach us that this sort of decision is never taken in the heaven of abstract principles. Life itself becomes our educator about life, a teacher whose lessons are always difficult and sometimes crucifying.

Where, to be more precise, is the place in life where our faith decisions are made? I will do no more than evoke, by way of illustration, two experiences in which everyone, I think, will recognize himself or herself. At the same time, the two are sufficiently different from each other to suggest "life lessons" that challenge our whole existence, in all its commitments and conflicts.

A Sick Body

Is there anything more banal than the flu? But when the flu attacks *us*, life is all at sixes and sevens. Our sinuses are plugged up, our throat inflamed, our limbs "weak and weary," the fever seems to rob our head of its normal capacity to function.

Above all, a bad case of the flu lessens our availability; it prevents us from being fully present to ourselves and to others. But then, during this detestable interlude, what becomes of the limitless love that Christians profess? We can hardly put up with ourselves! Do we have to wait before we return to health to begin loving ourselves again, as a son or daughter of God is called to love himself or herself? Even relations with the persons closest to us, parents, friends, coworkers, and so on, are handicapped. So do we have to momentarily forget our faith in the possibility of approaching others and welcoming them in a state of *perfect* openness? A bout with the flu is enough to show how a sick body limits our decisions and harasses our practice of salvation.

A case of the flu, in general, doesn't last long. We know we'll get over it. But what about an illness that tests us for a long, all too long, time—one that on some days becomes a faithful but unbearable companion? Here I'm going to run the risk of shamelessly talking about myself: For more than thirty years I have been sick with a disease that has gotten, and continues to get, worse. I don't want to ramble on, but what has this sickness taught me about faith in day-to-day practice? What is it always teaching me, as it stubbornly resists treatment and I find it so hard to get used to? I think that everyone in the grip of a long-lasting disease will agree that three great moments of awareness have a special status.

A sick body is always *there*, obstinately planting itself in the middle of life, to remind us that *we are limited beings.* This awareness of limits, many people will think, is obvious. I'd qualify that by saying that it should be obvious.

When everything goes relatively well, we are all more or less afflicted, it seems to me, by the superman or superwoman complex. So many needs prompt our sense of all the responsibilities we have. Aren't we really altogether indispensable? If, in addition, we believe that a universal love dwells within us and impels us toward others, then we will be inclined to take upon ourselves all the problems of the world. We run left and right, we can remain deaf to no appeal. Then we become indefatigable—and often exhausted missionaries. As the saying goes, aren't we all tempted to "take ourselves for the Good Lord"?

A sick body cools off this kind of ardor. To take but one small example, of its own accord it takes charge of a painful cleansing, it clears our agendas: It cancels meetings we wanted to attend, forbids commitments we have already made or would like to make, shortens or makes less frequent the precious moments of meeting others....

Thus, bit by bit, the experience of limits develops a second "take" of awareness, the awareness of what is called the *funnel effect*. And *that* may be the greatest of all sufferings.

At the top of the funnel, even when one is sick, nothing seems limited, everything appears immensely open. We are still full of the most beautiful desires, still inclined to cultivate them with care and to translate them into reality. The fire in our hearts has *not* gone out. There has been no diminishment in our thirst to love and be loved, nor in our appetite for working so that our world may be a little more brotherly and sisterly, a little more habitable for everyone. Sickness hasn't killed a certain faith in the absolute. Not yet, at any rate, we sometimes murmur to ourselves, as if in encouragement or longing.

But there's always that little tube at the base of the funnel. The narrowness of the tube…it resists the immensity of our desires, letting only a few of them filter through, condemning us to littleness, to small projects and small achievements. From time to time it gets completely blocked.

It's hard to manage one's relations with a sick body in a healthy fashion. In particular, how do we prevent the sickness from taking over the whole territory? Sick persons can't, they don't have the right to, exile themselves from the body and its limits. Here, too, they are called on to put their faith into practice. But, at the same time, the longer the sickness lasts, the more the sick body tends to want to invade all of life, to hog the stage, take up all the space. How can we not disappear, how can be not lose our own name in relations with ourselves and others? or with God? How can we be something else besides a sick body?

We wind up discovering that sickness attacks much more than the body. The person, the whole person, is threatened. Sickness wants to run the life of the sick person. Without constant vigilance one might gradually stop being a humane, responsible person and turn into an image, a mask, a "patient." How to say this (it's far from being a theoretical question)? Just think of the more or less subtle vacillations that render human relations so fragile at such times. In dealing with others, sick people are no longer quite themselves. Thanks to the sickness that has interposed itself, they feel strongly that others have to cover some distance to get where *they* are. Thus a sick person is invited to a third realization: *the need to fight isolation and tame one's solitude.*

It's often said that our world is smothering us beneath the weight of solitude. That's not true! It's isolation that rips apart the fabric of our personal and collective existence.

I don't yet have a very good idea of what solitude is. But one notion certainly keeps forcing itself upon me more and more: Solitude is full of life, it's swarming with people. It's the place where all of us, no longer afraid of our personal truth, including its limits, can take up residence; it has freed up an interior space and opens the heart; it allows us to move more freely toward others, with no desire to colonize them. It also permits us to let them inhabit us. I have even come to think that life has been given to us precisely for this reason—so that we can domesticate that solitude.

Isolation is not born of this sort of truth-work on ourselves and taming of ourselves. It is a locking up. It results from a game of masks, and this game leads to death. "The old," "the young," "welfare mothers," "homosexuals," "the unemployed," "immigrants": All these names are masks that we impose on others, on strangers that we isolate, the better to control our relations with them. It's easy to hide ourselves behind these masks, probably out of fear of our own vulnerability. All these masks choke off the real faces, so beautiful and so fragile, so beautiful in their fragility.

Sick persons must constantly struggle against the forces around them, but perhaps especially *in them*, that would like to condemn them to isolation. We are so very alone in a sick body. But we must never consent to being just a "patient." Rather, we must always affirm ourselves as a "human being who is sick." One must constantly pass from isolation to solitude.

∞

A long illness radicalizes a number of questions to which a simple case of the flu has already provided an introduction. At certain times, it serves as a special challenge to faith in God. Where has God gone? People professed their faith in him as a tender and loving God, always concerned with bringing life to birth. Yet sickness appears to be the opposite of life. Instead of celebrating the promises of a birth, it pursues a long labor of decay; it gradually extinguishes the energies of the body, the mind, or both at the same time.

Philosopher André Comte-Sponville was once asked: "What are the reasons, nowadays, for not believing in God?" His answer: "The first and strongest reason is the existence and immensity of evil[…]How can one imagine that a God has willed the diseases, the suffering of children, the decrepitude of old people?"[3] Sick people don't simply note the sufferings and decrepitude around them. These are things that the sick person is living in himself or herself. But where, then, has God gone?

Christian faith confesses the beauty and the pride of the sons and daughters of God. "Arise and walk." The heaviness of a sick body hardly prompts us to take to the road again. How can we decide to put a universal love into practice when sickness increasingly restrains our energies, when it pares down everything, even the possibility of approaching others and placing ourselves concretely at their service?

When sickness hits hard, and bids fair to last, it's cold comfort to hear people telling us that there is light at the end of the tunnel. Sick persons aren't passengers on a train. They aren't flying along rails that mechanically guarantee their exit from the tunnel. That's how somewhere in me is etched the near-desperation I felt one evening. It was around six o'clock. I had to go to the lecture hall in an hour. One thought obsessed me: How can I go to talk about life when my mouth tastes nothing but ashes?

The Weaknesses of Love

Poets have the gift of expressing in a few words the essential things of life. Four lines are enough for Gilles Vigneault to voice the power and the weaknesses of human love:

Remember to forget
That it's never the same hour.
I love you, and I remain here
At the top of the staircase.

At the center of this poem, resounding like a cry is: *I love you*. Wedged in between two phrases that take more time to unpack is a cry that, in its brevity, wants to say everything. Long demonstrations would not affirm any more, or any better, the *absolute* status of love. They would only water it down, lose it in the mazes of an all-too-rational wisdom. Love can't explain itself; it has no need to. It's just there, beyond reason, a certitude truer than any truth requiring a long proof: *I love you*! Lovers are seized by love as if by an irresistible force. It makes you "lose your reason," "not know what to say," writes Jean Ferrat, echoing the words of poet Louis Aragon.

Some people have the impression that love, when it comes down on us, can be lived out only in the mode of *fusion*. It's as if one's whole life were to be concentrated in the cry, "I love you." Love lays hold of two beings and "concentrates" them so as to make them into one. Countless songs just play variations on the theme, "I am you, you are me, we are one."

But, deep down, the poet isn't fooled. The absolute force of his "I love you" seems to be cramped between two phrases that give us a hint of its weakness. A double weakness, inscribed as it is in *time* and *space*. The lover would prefer to pass over this weakness in silence. But he knows or suspects that it threatens the sense of fullness that has taken hold of him.

Love as fusion seems too strong and sturdy to ever be quenched someday. So it will be victorious over *time*; it bears within itself its own promises of eternity. How could it envisage an eventual crumbling away? "Our love will span time, *all* time. It's forever."

None of that prevents the lover from exhorting or begging, "Remember to forget that it's never the same time...." Because time passes and flies. How can we know or be sure that it won't bring with it the exhaustion of our love? "Forget that time passes and that, in its long and slow passage, our love is in danger of gradually being extinguished." Love feels itself and wants itself to be eternal. But will it really be able to resist the wear and tear of everyday life, of passing time, of the hours and years that it wants to traverse? Will it know how—without thereby ceasing to remain young—to express itself over the long haul? We would like to stop time and thus exorcise the menace that time constitutes for the absolute claims of love. Still, no one can forget that "It's never the same hour." Love can believe itself irresistible and unconquerable all it wants; it will still have to resist familiarization, it will have to conquer the lazy habits that would stifle its absolute desires.

A second weakness of human love is that we can't lock it up in a *space* that would protect it against the outside. Here, once more, we have to listen to what the love songs say. Many of them, for example, dream of an island where the lovers, the only inhabitants of that closed space, would no longer have to face attacks from the "world outside."

Vigneault sounds more prosaic: "I love you, and I remain here / at the top of the staircase." But whether one tries to gather together all space "at the top of the staircase" or in the exotic setting of a remote island, the intention is the same: Love has to protect itself against what lies elsewhere, the dangers that come from somewhere else. Perhaps "elsewhere" conceals attractions that one or the other of the lovers won't be able to resist. "If you go away from me, what guarantee do we have left of our fidelity? If you were only to take a few steps outside—or travel thousands of miles away—who or what can assure me beyond all doubt that you won't meet someone there more lovable and attractive than me, someone who will come to steal our love?"

Vigneault is well aware that no human being can install himself permanently at the top of a staircase. He would dry up there, and so he would infallibly cause the death of the very love that he wanted to protect. But when the absolute force of love seizes hold of us, we arm ourselves as best we can! Even the most ridiculous exorcisms seem like a good defense against everything that, viewed from the outside, might drain the superabundance that we are living through.

∽

At its birth, and in its tender youth, love finds little difficulty in *putting itself into practice*. If it undergoes constraints and has to struggle against them, it believes that they're external. One fights against outside forces. As for itself, it drinks at the wellspring of its own dynamism, it feeds on its own plenitude. How could it feel the demands of *decision making*? The lovers have been seized. All they have to do is let themselves be borne up on the waves of that seizure, since its plenitude is so generous in promising the inexhaustible rediscovery of their gestures of tenderness.

Love as fusion can't imagine, or at least it has a hard time imagining, that the bonds of love might some day break. "You are too much me, I am too much you," it likes to tell itself. "Nothing can separate us." We are sure that love is all-powerful. It will let the lovers lose themselves one in the other forever and find at last in that blessed loss the secret of a love that is always young.

Nevertheless, the days come when by a sort of fatality already built into everyone's body, a distance begins to form. Life teaches love that it has no future if, to nourish itself, it should demand that everyone wipe out his or her originality. Then one is forced to recognize that "I am unique, and you are unique. I'm not you, and I never could be you. You aren't me, and you have to stop wanting to become me." Thus love learns that it won't be able to survive, much less grow, on the ruins of persons who have ceased to be free and so have ceased to be persons.

Despite the dream that energized our life, we have discovered that it's impossible to dissolve ourselves completely one into the other. And if one has *identified* love with fusion, if one can't conceive any other kind of love except of the fusion variety, how not conclude that love is dead when the feeling of fusion has faded? So many couples break up when love has stopped being blindingly clear, an irresistible power that one need only obey.

Still it's not certain that love has died along with the thrusts toward fusion. And wouldn't the true blinding be to refuse the appeals that life then makes to love? Perhaps love is being invited to convert, to see itself and live itself differently. It is already dead, really dead, if *the bond* between the two persons reveals itself to be incapable of *serving everyone's quest to become free.* But to serve that sort of becoming, love has to die to its needs of fusion and to translate itself into work, into a task that is never done once and for all.

Without ceasing to be a gift to be received, love, of itself, defines the challenges of its being put into practice. It is given, but it also depends on our response to the needs, always difficult and constraining, of a responsible decision. Our birth to love is gratis. But life teaches us that we are equally responsible for our loves. We must constantly *decide* to *become* lovers.

2

Deciding to Do
What Is Possible

Christian faith is not a poultice that one applies to existence, to one's problems and wounds, so as to numb the pain of life. Out of loyalty to Jesus Christ and to his Incarnation, what we believe has to be put into practice right in the middle of existence, of our entire existence, including poverty and wounds.

Christian women and men have to recenter themselves *yes* here on the person of Jesus Christ. It is to this person and his mystery that our attitudes and behavior, our talk about death lived from day to day, directly send us. And Jesus didn't want to play tricks with death, so much so that he didn't die "a natural death." That "terminal death" tells us a great deal about the grappling that he went through every day with the powers of death.

The whole existence of Jesus, in fact, had been consecrated to the revelation of a God of tenderness, a God who engenders, a God whose sole concern is to bring humans to birth and rebirth in freedom. If Jesus ends his life on a cross, if he leaves his last breath there, that is because of his everyday fidelity to this project: He revealed a God who destabilized and threatened too many of the powers that be, especially the political and religious powers. The meaning of his history as a man, and of all the deaths he confronted daily so as to be faithful to it; all that surely enters, somehow or another, into the "definition" of salvation—and hence of the life to which Christian faith invites us.

So Christians can't speak of the Resurrection of Jesus Christ as if it were *independent* of his terminal death and of all his "daily" deaths of which the New Testament provides us an account. That Resurrection does not become, and in the first place not for Jesus, a sort of "point zero" in a new life. No one can understand it as an absolute beginning that henceforth renders insignificant the human existence of Jesus and somehow discredits his own struggles with limits and suffering, with the deaths that he had to live through all during his life.

Everything has not been said—far from it—on the sicknesses and weaknesses of life. But I would think the preceding pages are enough to show some essential aspects of all practice of salvation, of all decisions in which the disciples risk the fate of their fidelity to the words of Jesus.

The putting into practice of salvation must be poor enough to come to terms with the limits of human existence.

Sick people know only too well the omnipresence of limits. Lovers always discover it too soon. But no one, whoever she is or whatever she does, can escape this burden of limits when, to avoid collapse and "total ruin," she decides to put her faith into practice. No one. Not the parents who would be everything and do everything for their children, but are always constrained in their desires, if only by the narrowness of their financial capacities. Not the teacher who is eager to arm his or her students for the future and is so often disarmed by them, by a new language and a new culture that he or she finds alien. Not the union members who struggle to better their working and living conditions, but keep on running up against "outside" economic interest of which they are too often the victims. Not the man or woman who has gone into politics the way one "enters religion" (some messiahs quickly get disenchanted by the meager room in which they have to maneuver).

Everyone has to take a good look at his or her life. The list of one's limits will perhaps be a long one, and easier to make, than the list of reasons for optimism and letting go.

Limits exist and come into play within everyone; within myself they prepare the arena of "putting into practice."

Especially at the beginning of a commitment, how can we not spontaneously look upon limits as realities *external* to ourselves? At that point they are, to be sure, easier to identify. They mark off a battlefield, but the struggle is fought with something or someone who is outside us. It's as if we had an unlimited interior, untouched and untouchable: That would be the realm of faith, confronting the threats from outside. Meanwhile, faith itself would remain safe, always safe, miraculously protected.

But no one can decide to put his faith into practice, if he limits himself to ascertaining the limits facing him from the outside. The truth-work leads us to move gradually, almost underhandedly, from the verb "to have" (I *have* limits) to the verb "to be" (I *am* limited).

My body, for example, causes me to occupy a small, restricted space. Despite my faith in *universal* brotherhood, I cannot exist as a believing person anywhere except in actions that are always narrowly *personal*. Even if I hear the calls for commitment that I might validly pursue elsewhere, I can't be everywhere at the same time. I can't be both in the Third World and my own country, at work and with my children, in Congress and doing continuous service for those less privileged than myself, and so forth.

We know that we have been visited by a love without boundaries of any sort. Still, wanting to be everywhere at the same time is the most convenient excuse for men and women who lack the courage to be *anywhere in particular.*

So it is necessary that the disciples of Jesus Christ lucidly and bravely measure the limits that define their life and what they are. Otherwise, to whom will they be truly faithful? to Jesus Christ? Their practice will answer that question of itself, because they won't have to endure the poverty of putting salvation into practice in a specific place, in service to a definite situation. Under the pretext of faith, I can pretend to be everything and to do everything. In practice, I won't really exist *anywhere*.

For every disciple who wishes to put the words of Jesus into practice, no faith-decision is "chemically pure."

We have to dare to repeat our decision every day, because the health of our Christian life depends so much upon it: Christ himself wants to be situated in our *freedom in action,* in our *decisions*.[4]

Out of fidelity to the Incarnation, we are forced to make a major adjustment—a difficult one—but, we hope, a liberating one, too, to cleanse our faith of all the strictly idealistic visions that we might entertain. If *we are* limited, there is no place in us that would be *the* site of faith, that would permit fully human decisions that would be at the same time free of all limits.

Parents, children, politicians, spouses, unmarried persons, teachers: Whatever we are, whatever we wish to invest, to put into practice somewhere, is truly faith's absolute. But no one has the right to claim that his or her decision is unlimited. Let us plainly translate into reality the desires of the God of Jesus Christ for us and our commitments.

Who wouldn't love to be, in some "place" of his or her being, in direct communication with the Holy Spirit? It would be like having a telephone connecting us with Jesus Christ and allowing us to know what decision to make in any given situation. It's often in the most difficult moments, however, and when we launch our most pressing and urgent appeals, that God seems to turn deaf and dumb. "If he could clearly reveal the decision I should make...." But then would it still be a human decision of someone responsible for what he or she does?

"A disciple is not above the teacher" (Matthew 10:24). Jesus himself stumbled against the heavy silence of God: "My God, my God, why have you forsaken me?" (Matthew 27:46). In this painful question we find concentrated and revealed the truth of Jesus' Incarnation. He was and remained a free man until the end of his days, even if he, like all human beings, had to pay a high price for the decisions made by such freedom.

Throughout the time of our lives, we must decide to commit our faith in actions that are humanly possible for us.

Here is something that seems to contradict everything I managed to argue in my earlier book on the relations between Christian faith and human pride.

Pride (in the good sense), I said then, feeds on one certitude: Jesus Christ makes the impossible possible. He has merited, he promises and guarantees, a full love of oneself and of others. And even, we believe, a full love of God. A full love means a perfect love, absolute and unlimited. Here is where Jesus Christ himself, inviting his disciples to put his words into practice, sends them off to their freedom. To decisions taken daily that, unless they are taken on as always limited decisions, will change nothing in life and will never transform it according to the words of Jesus.

An illness that momentarily disorients us or, much more roughly, nails us to the bed for good; a love that wants to be eternal and can't even find the words and gestures to express itself correctly today; a commitment to politics, a field that has been correctly defined as the "art of the possible"; and so on. How can we continue to believe in a freedom capable of the impossible when life teaches that such freedom is limited and can do no more than what is possible?

As we might already guess, whoever decides to put love into practice keeps going forth to meet death. From one death to death on a daily basis. Such death makes us frightened, which is normal. We would prefer to pass it by. Sometimes we do everything so as not to have to engage in hand-to-hand combat with it. Would we be worthy of human existence if we were to refuse to live it?

Part Two

Many-Faced Death

*T*o do what is possible... Put that way, it sounds so easy. It's like an invitation to slackness: "Let yourself glide on the wave of the days, recalling above all that *no one is bound to do the impossible.*"

But Christian women and men are crazy enough to confess that the impossible has become possible. Would they still be real believers if they didn't care anymore about a love that is accomplished, offered, and already possible? And what if they were no longer bound to put it into practice on the level of their human decisions? In truth we believe that all of us are bound to do the impossible.

Deep down, it isn't the absolute status of faith that causes the problem. No one can live without an absolute, of whatever nature, drawing us on and keeping us, humanly speaking, alive. It is no longer the limits of our bodies and our loves that, all by themselves, report about the pain we feel in living. Who of us hasn't learned that our little decisions single-handedly produce commitments that will make our today breathe, enough for it to continue on the march and to consent to move toward tomorrow and the day after? What makes existence hard is the *collision*, in our everyday lives, between the absolute and limits.

Our decisions, then, have to respond to a double fidelity: to the God of Jesus Christ and to our own limits. This is an uncomfortable situation, from which we can

29

never completely escape. But our lives must show that faith doesn't condemn us to two contradictory loyalties. Our *lives*—not our words, our speeches, or our theories.

That is how we set out, day after day, to meet death.

3
Clearing the Horizon

A very close friend of mine, a man who was then the father of two young children, had joined a group of MarxistLeninists. This was back in the years of the grand revolutionary dreams. Driven by a thirst for justice (which, by the way, has never left him), my friend found in his militancy what he needed to satisfy his aspirations. But he also loved his wife and his children....Too bad for him, I would add, since things have been spoiled ever since the day that certain pure-minded and hardheaded persons began to attack him on that front. They told him that the time he spent with his family was wasted; it was time stolen from "the cause." He had to break out.

No "cause" is worth burying our entire life in—even God, if God is no more than a cause to defend. All fanatics, including the god-fanatics, claim they are flying to rescue human freedom. In fact, they threaten to kill that freedom. And they have, by the way, literally done too much killing. They are still, even today, killing too many.

A cause doesn't *pro*pose, it *im*poses itself. Rather than opening up to freedom a field of possible decisions, it shrinks freedom's horizon, it shanghais and asphyxiates people. So it moves in a direction opposite to the one that Jesus proposes to his disciples.

The God of Jesus Christ wants to be situated in the *becoming* of every person and every community.[5] If that's the case, how can we use God as a pretext for justifying a confinement of freedom? In truth, our first responsibility might well be to respect the *opening* to which the God of Jesus Christ invites our existence. We are constantly invited to reopen the "fan," the gamut of our humanly possible decisions.

I think that our life is much more capable of opening up than we are inclined to believe. Even in the darkest moments, in days as black as night, even when our freedom seems so alienated that the whole horizon appears to be blocked off. After a certain amount of time, and if we continue to care to be and to act like responsible persons, a little decision ends up proving to be a decision that is *possible today*—a decision that, despite its apparent smallness, gives a bit of future to the present.

Love of oneself, love of others, and, for believers, love of God are three relationships that we have the responsibility to keep open. How can we concretely carry out this work of opening? No one can answer that for anyone else, first of all because no one is in charge of the questions that others ask themselves. If I let myself share a few questionings, that's only to invite all of us *not to block off the horizon of possible decisions too soon.*

Becoming myself, learning to love myself, is a task that demands a vigilant attention to the decisions that it's possible for me to make and that will keep me alive. Does my life seem too full for me to take care of my body? Before it's too late, I have to set up a space for physical exercise and relaxation. I have to get a good look at what is concretely possible and, above all, to move on to practice, if only, for example, by deciding to spend a certain amount of time walking to work. Is that work so monopolizing that it wipes out even the possibility of "wasting time" with the people who are the most important to me? For a long time a couple who are friends of mine went out almost every Sunday to have coffee at a restaurant. Far from the house and the children, it was their special moment. After thirty years of marriage, they are glad they faithfully stuck to their little ritual; it was so simple, but something that was concretely possible for them.

We can think, in a wider context, of how the condition of women has evolved in the present day. Not so long ago the only prospect available to most women was to stay and work at home. Today countless women are discovering that there are other possibilities. With the help of certain rearrangements in the life of the couple and the family—but still too often at the price of almost superhuman efforts—they can think about earning money through work outside the house and even about pursuing careers once forbidden to them.

This exercise in openness must be pursued in our relations with others. Poverty is proliferating. Are the "poor"
beginning to get on my nerves or, perhaps, to threaten
my security? What if I took the time to do a little analysis: What is creating this galloping poverty? What are its
causes? Or again, at the risk of being hurt by the experience, couldn't I expose myself to *certain* poor people?
Couldn't I let their life, so often unlivable, get through to
me, at least to some small extent? Perhaps I don't understand the life, so different from mine, that homosexuals
lead. But I probably know *one* of them, someone who
would agree to share with me a little of what he or she is
and how he or she lives, and who would prevent me from
locking myself up in lethal prejudices. Even relations with
the most distant others are becoming radically transformed, if only because of prodigious developments in
the electronic means of communication. But can I be sat-
isfied with knowing these others from a video screen when
there undoubtedly are immigrants around and near me
who would embody the distant world that the image si-
multaneously brings close and keeps far away?

Our relations with God call for as much vigilance as
the first two. Even more, no doubt, since our days are
always chock-full: "I'll take care of it when I've finished
with the most pressing items...." Am I tempted to join
large movements that, these days, want to discredit all
real work of intelligence and faith? In the extreme form
of this view and slightly caricaturing it, the idea would
be that the more of a simpleton one is in the domain of

faith, the more one would be a real believer. Do I know
how to profit from the countless means available (books,
lectures, courses, discussion groups, and so on) that will
prevent me from falling prey to a desiccating fundamen-
talism? And, again, do I know how to find moments for
prayer?

In a little community that a group of us has made up
for some fifteen years, this question comes up so often
that we have more or less chosen to laugh at it. Everyone
sees that relations with oneself and others are nurtured
and changed by such moments of prayer. All of us have
tried to reserve a space that regularly leaves room for
them. But everyone realizes, sooner or later, that the arrangements made a short time ago are no longer viable
today. Jostled and hustled by family life, job, and leisure
activities, each one of us has quite simply "forgotten"
those useless but necessary moments and has to reinvent
other arrangements.

One last question: In a world that has become very
demanding about competence and efficiency, have I come
to judge myself solely in terms of measurable productiv-
ity? If so, it is more than time to give a chance to the
desires that live in me but get stifled. In particular, for a
believer, this means the desires for a God whose love is
freely given and invites a free gift. The taste of freedom
gets lost when we are wholly taken up with fulfilling our
own needs and the needs of those around us, when we no
longer even enjoy the leisure of allowing the loveliest desires to emerge and be cared for.

We could pursue this sort of questioning indefinitely. What's important and necessary here is that every person grasp the purpose of such an exercise and take it up regularly for himself or herself. *Let no one close off the horizon of his or her freedom too soon.* As Gilles Vigneault writes:

The flowers of the time for loving
Have never bloomed in a sealed-up heart
Night day summer winter
You have to sleep with your heart open.

"To sleep with your heart open" also means to make an honest effort to name the decisions that are possible for *me* today. Otherwise, how can we remain alive, put the gospel into practice, and work concretely for our own liberation?

4
Everyday Deaths

*E*ven if we have to remain constantly attentive to possible decisions, the openness of our existence is not unlimited. We might wish things were different. Sometimes we indulge in the illusion that it isn't so. But just as we barely manage to scrape by when we neglect to reopen the fan of possibilities, so the failure to respect limits disembodies and sterilizes freedom.

If we try, on the other hand, to live convivially with our limits, they take it upon themselves to remind us of an essential law of existence: The yesses of our decisions always imply noes; they demand a renunciation. Their vigor even depends on the vigor with which we can say the noes that every decision requires. "Let your 'Yes' be 'yes' and your 'No' be 'no'" (James 5:12). In a word, *no one can live free without renunciation.*

A Renunciation That Is Submission and Resignation

"Renounce"—what an outmoded word! When I used to speak about renunciation to college students, their first reaction was to resist the idea, to close up, or reject it straight-out. It takes a certain daring or a great deal of naiveté these days to address a topic with such a loaded past.

It seems to me that I have some small notion of this sort of resistance and rejection. The invitation to renunciation has looked very much like an incitement to self-contempt, to an alienating and alienated masochism. Even today, don't people generally understand renunciation along lines that run counter to everything that I've managed to say about Christian pride?

This movement is characterized, first of all and above all, by legalism, voluntarism, and conformism. Something has to be said about this. Fidelity to Jesus Christ urges us to do so, just as much as our love of human existence.

The refusal of legalism, I want to specify from the outset, is not an infantile refusal of the law. No human group can live without laws. Furthermore, no human being can live free without providing himself or herself with a certain framework. The question that I raise concerns, rather, the *relations* between laws and liberty: Does the law serve us, does it serve our freedom, or do we serve the law? We shouldn't be too quick to respond that the question is simplistic and the answer obvious....

When we ask ourselves about the relations between law and liberty, our interest must be directed to a *movement*, to a *dynamic*.

At the outset of the dehumanizing approach to voluntarist renunciation, someone somewhere posited a law (moral, social, religious) defining *a priori* the frontiers between an inside and an outside, between the pure and the impure. That someone could, by the way, very well be ourselves, since our need for security aspires to a life that is correct, well ordered, and clearly framed, sheltered from all unwelcome surprises.

So it is not the freedom of the children of God that comes first, in the beginning of the whole movement. It's the law, with its clear-cut rigidity, its serene assurance of defining the "true truth" of life. *Then* the demand is made that persons or social groups conform to the law, and not go wandering outside the permissible boundary lines, in the troubled space of the forbidden.

If I have enough strength or rigidity not to go outside to taste forbidden fruits, if I have the courage to *renounce* what the law forbids, *then* I will be someone respectable, then I will be beautiful. To put matters in Christian terms: I will be able to call myself a faithful disciple of Jesus Christ *after* my firm renunciation of what the law forbids—and as soon as I have *conformed* to the law and the rules. My beauty, in other words, comes from conformity.

Thus renunciation, according to this sort of connection between law and liberty, means submitting to laws that determine our fidelity in advance. The more one clings to a rigid observance of the law, however, the less room there is for questioning, searching, seeking errors along the way, doubt.

I have spoken at length about the Christian life in terms of genesis and evolution.[6] But how can we be conscious of, and responsible for, our free development when we have refused the conditions that are essential to all becoming? What happens when questions, errors, and doubts are all *a priori* forbidden?

In this perspective, renunciation is quite concretely equal to resignation, resigning myself into the hands of those who have defined the laws, are the guardians of the laws, and judge my fidelity or infidelity to them. Of course, I can play this role with myself, for example, when I let a familiar, comfortable way of life handle the job of shaping the present and future paths of my fidelity.

That is how all the god-fanatics I was talking about above show their contempt for both God and human freedom. God has become a cause to defend, something one undertakes to squeeze into a constricting network of laws and norms. And human fidelity gets degraded into conformity with the law. Still, "the letter kills, but the Spirit gives life" (2 Corinthians 3:6).

Daily Decisions and Everyday Renunciations

The renunciation that I wish to—that I have to—speak about corresponds to a completely different dynamic. Far from persecuting freedom and alienating us, it permits decisions that will be real decisions.

I don't say perfectly free decisions, since in our world there is no such thing as chemically pure freedom. I am talking about "true" decisions, that is, decisions that really decide something.

Every disciple who is truly concerned with putting into practice the words of Jesus is called to bring into being full love in the practices that are humanly possible for him or her. That is why, wishing to live my faith somewhere, at this or that moment of my existence, in response to this or that challenge facing me, *my faith-decision can only be limited.* This is precisely where renunciation awaits me—not in submission to a predefined law, but *in the very act of my decision to live.*

All that may seem terribly abstract. Still, we live it every day, even in the decisions that appear to be of little importance.

Every night I come home, worn out by a day of especially trying work. My children are in a hurry to see me. They call for my presence and attention. I can lie down and try to recoup a minimum of energy, something that might strike me as totally legitimate. Or I can respond, or at least try to respond, to the demands of the children, which might be equally legitimate. What to decide? One thing is certain: I can't allow myself to rest up and at the same time be an active presence with the children. So I can't decide in favor of a possible choice without deciding to *renounce* the other choice. And it *is* a question of my faith-decision, my freedom as a believer who must commit himself or herself everywhere, including gestures that seem awfully banal. Let us add, further, that my renunciation will do harm (even if the wound is superficial and temporary), regardless of whether I give up the restorative sleep or the turbulent but loving presence of the children.

A woman friend who is the mother of five children always views the coming of Christmas with apprehension. Having lived in a Third World country, she knows the immense suffering caused by poverty. She also knows the inestimable value of real solidarity, and she would like to introduce her children to a sense of sharing. But Christmastime finds our society playing the game of shameless overconsumption. An adult can easily resist it, but what child could escape the barrage of ads that assails him or her from all sides? "If your parents love you, it's normal to get lots of presents for Christmas," say or imply the publicity experts. "And this year you have to have this and that and the other thing. Your friends will have it...." What to do? How can parents struggle against such potent forms of pressure? Besides, won't the children feel marginalized if they don't get what their friends have? It will be necessary to say no, without being absolutely sure that the no won't traumatize the children to the point that our concern with educating them might produce an effect opposite to the one looked for. When children are involved—one's own children—decisions and renunciation are always difficult.

Our life grows or wastes away depending on the decisions, most often little ones, that we make or refuse to make during the twenty-four hours of each day. And the same is true of the renunciations demanded by our decisions. These renunciations, without which our lives go slack, no longer have the edge without which we ultimately become incapable of deciding anything.

Saying No by Deciding to Say Yes

One day, during a major housecleaning, I chose not to throw out the lists of things to do that I had drawn up in my first years of work. It wasn't as if I wanted to save some traces of the good old days, or savor the pleasure of emotional investments that had paid off. Rather, it was to keep a reminder of what I can and must no longer do. How indispensable I thought I was, trying to be everywhere just a little. Incapable of regretting anything, I still wonder: *Have I fought well enough against an unhealthy messianism, too proud to consent to the limits of every even slightly serious and sustained commitment?* In a word, have I known how to consent to *my* possibilities?

Without this sort of consent, it's a good bet that I'm living and spreading an unhealthy idealism. As Maurice Bellet notes so rightly: "Thus, if I decide, I have to decide *this*: apart from this, one takes a flight into the sublime. And so, what can I decide except, precisely, what's possible for me?"[7]

What do Bellet's words mean? First of all, I can't decide to make Christian love exist in *this* at the same time as in that—and that and that as well. I can't, for example, be a full-time professor, a good servant of the students for whom I'm responsible, while pursuing multiple activities, each of which would demand a full-time commitment. I can't be *here* and there and there and there as well, floating everywhere without being able to take root and really exist somewhere. I can't be so concerned with everyone in general that it would become practically impossible for me to love someone in particular or to look after those particular loves for which I am immediately responsible: my wife, my children, or those persons whom I have won over, who have won me over, and whom I can't just let drop.

In saying yes to our role as God's sons and daughters, we are driven to say yes to a universal love. That is why no one has the right to close off too soon the field of possible commitments, to impose on her heart and her hands boundaries that are too rapidly fixed.

A second demand, however, has also been formulated. In virtue of our faith in the Incarnation, we profess our belief in a God who respects our limits, who loves them, who loves us in our limits. How, in the very name of the God we believe in, can we not enter (at least a little) into the movement of his tenderness? How not be tender toward our limits, which are *ourselves*? The God of Jesus Christ expects from us a second yes, which is the loving consent to our personal and collective limits.

One and the same act of faith affirms that I am ca-

pable of the impossible, even as it forbids me to take myself
for God. Here, then, is how faith itself, if it is Christian,
urges me to recognize that *everything isn't always possible for me.*

Each day I must give breath to my life by opening up a
large enough space so that my choices can be named.
Each day, too, I have to decide *this*—and so die to all the
theoretically possible *thats* which the truth and vigor of
my decision remove from me, *dying to all the possible
choices that become, for me, concretely impossible.* We
see that it's not always so simple and easy to "do what is
possible."

5
The Burden of the Impossible

I don't want to talk about big deaths or little deaths. Since everything is at stake in freedom in actions, in decisions, who am I to test the weight of my own freedom? Who am I to judge the true burden of the decisions for which others are responsible? Who am I to determine the heaviness of their limits? Can I measure their sufferings, the death with which they are fighting, the griefs that they have to traverse as freely as possible? On that score life often takes it upon itself to surprise us and to lead us to a greater poverty. The freedom of such and such a person or group of persons seems to me completely stifled; and then, look, it proves to be capable of the impossible. Some other person or people would appear to have everything needed to play the serious game of decision-making, and yet they apparently delight in irresponsibility. But who am I to arrogate the power of sounding the depths of the heart?

Still, it seems to me that one can still add two refinements here. And although they won't allow us to evaluate freedom the way one measures an object, they will help us to understand better (and especially, we must hope, to live better) our grappling with death.

The heavier the limits of our lives, we must first specify, the more the field of concretely possible choices shrinks.

It's not because a family barely secures its daily bread that it turns a deaf ear to the invitation to leave for a vacation: They are quite aware of the billboard posters, the newspaper and television ads, all those broadcast appeals that are so many reminders of their feeble financial capacities and of a possibility that's not possible for them. At the same time that governments invite bosses and unions to a dialogue, "economic rationality" is closing factories, eliminating jobs, and creating jobless workers who have no say in the decisions that land on their heads. It's easy to rationalize the economy when the anticipated profits will come to swell already-full pockets. For the unemployed, the horizon is closed off. A people subjected to a dictatorial regime dreams of freedom. What are the concrete margins for maneuvering, in its struggle to promote and restore the institutions that will guarantee some space for individual and collective freedoms? What are its real possibilities?

On the subject of an illness that promises to last and is

progressively worsening, I spoke above of the funnel-effect. The sick person continues to dream "the impossible dream" that Jacques Brel sang about. But when the time for decision comes, the fan of possible choices closes dangerously: How many "noes" have to be lived through, how many have to be taken on! The field of commitments diminishes bit by bit, autonomy is lost, we have to renounce the activities that nourished our joy in life. Some people even end up wondering if joy is still possible, since no sparkle of it manages to surface, to pass through the thickness of the limits. Where will this degradation leave the body and the heart?

And what to say about psychologically wounded persons, who have been deeply hurt, sometimes battered and bruised, at a very young age? They include, for example, those who haven't been loved or have been loved badly. They, too, have the right to dream the impossible dream of a love without limits. They have the right to love. What pain for them not to know if their wounds will heal one day and if love will finally visit them! Still worse, perhaps, what pain for them not to be sure that they themselves will become capable of loving, and of loving well! Will the moment of grace come when the free gift of welcome will be possible for them? While waiting for that moment, they live through the present as the It has to be added—and this will be the second refinement: The more profoundly a decision engages the freedom of everyone concerned, the more it gives a sort of depth to the yeses and the noes that we are responsible for.

Throughout these pages I have used a formula that might seem exaggerated or, at most, good for causing a shock: No one can decide to live without deciding to die. I hope I have made it sufficiently clear that this formula holds for all the decisions that we make day after day. It remains to be seen whether we will apply it more seriously to our most fundamental decisions.

Among these decisions, doubtless the most serious is that of becoming oneself. For a Christian, God himself wants to depend on that original, unique becoming for which nobody except each one of us can assume responsibility.[8]

But what noes we have to take on when we wish to say a real yes to ourselves! What renunciations and what deaths we have to live! I have to dwell within myself while saying no to the artificial charms of egoism, to the attractions of confinement in oneself. I have to constantly set off toward others while dying to the desire for fusion, without melting into them, without losing my identity in them. Poor and available, I have to welcome them into my life, not just to satisfy my needs but also to hear the word, the original (and upsetting!) word, that they have to say to me. I have to commit myself socially, in politics or elsewhere, even if that means both renouncing the warmth of a pleasant cocoon and dying to my appetite for the power to control. I have to be someone whose convictions remain clear and firm, spanning time, without becoming transformed into enslavement to a "cause" that may promise a certain gratification, but would be dehumanizing for me and for others. I have to say a yes to God that respects him as the Totally Other without making an idol out of him, a yes that will honor his infinite respect for my own freedom.

Death, with its many faces, awaits me at each turning in my life. How am I to become myself if I refuse the challenges that it flings at me?

Among the great and serious decisions of our existence one must also number what are called the "life choices." These are options with which one hopes to engage one's existence for a long time and, if possible, to span the whole duration of one's life. Here again, quite clearly, no one can decide to live without deciding to die.

I can't, for example, decide in favor of marriage, committing myself to a long-lasting union and swearing fidelity to someone "for life," without deciding to die to a way of acting, to attitudes and behaviors that characterize my life as a bachelor. What will become of my relationship to my spouse if I find time for everyone except her, if I can't give up for lost the commitments, leisure-time activities, and trips outside that lead me everywhere except to her side? What's the use of my plans and my decision if I flirt with all the women whom I find attractive?

"Why love only one woman when one could love a thousand?" asks Don Juan who, thanks to an intuition that originally was authentic, rushes headlong against the barriers of finitude; [he sees] eternity escaping in the multiplicity of instants when he wanted to conjure it up."[9]

The "authentic intuition" was "I am capable of an un-limited love." But the truth of my life-project demands a decision for a particular, limited love, without which my project is doomed to death and will dissolve in the scat-tering of multiple meetings and successive conquests.

Besides, a couple can't decide on bringing a child into their life without throwing that life into disorder, with-out the spouses having to decide to die to a one-on-one existence in which they were comfortably installed. Now they have to give up that comfort. Almost everything has to be rearranged: Sleep time is shortened, their bodies slump with fatigue, going out alone becomes increasingly rare, getting together with friends proves to be harder and harder. Happiness is there, but at the price of count-less renunciations, of deaths on a daily basis. Further-more, this commitment promises to last a long time, even if it is called over the years to be lived out in different ways. The parents, in fact, can hope that their children, once they become young adults, will no longer need them and will fly with their own wings. But who can say ex-actly when the responsibility of parents for their children has really, concretely come to an end?

Obviously persons who opt for celibacy don't escape this burden of the impossible that every life-choice cre-ates—always assuming, of course, that their celibacy is deliberate, as freely chosen as possible.

I bear no grudge against the priests who introduced me to what people have agreed to call "religious life." They did what they could with the means they had at the time. Nonetheless I'm aware of the sort of spiritualizing idealism in which our training, especially our preparation for a life of celibacy, was immersed.

"Eunuchs for the sake of the Kingdom of Heaven" (see Matthew 19:12), we were invited to die to Woman. An easy renunciation, especially since Woman doesn't exist. It's something else again, with heavier implications, to decide on a way of life where a woman will always be absent. Then one has to die to the presence of a person who might have been there, but never will be. A person with whom one might make one's way in a type of irreplaceable intimacy, discovering with her aspects of love that the celibate has to give up for lost. No one ever told me about that absence, that emptiness, or that death.

I don't want to discredit celibacy. I'm only saying that persons who have chosen celibacy as a lifetime project, if they want their choice to be a liberating one, have to be aware of what they are renouncing and have to take on the death that their decision implies. Otherwise, to use another expression formulated above, instead of making life, they risk sowing death in and around themselves.[10] The community life of religious, for example, can very well become the site of an affective blackmail, in which any given member of the community, insecure about his celibacy, waits for the others to fill up a void that they can't fill up. Each and every one, including the community as a community, comes off the loser.

Part Three

Death Work

*W*e constantly live with the burden of the impossible, of which I have just spoken. And day after day we have to struggle with the death that this impossibility provokes. When we speak of death, however, our spontaneous reactions and usual language almost always refer us to a sort of final point of earthly existence. I have had an example of this in mind ever since I began writing this book: It does me no good to tell the persons I'm talking to about my concern for death lived on a daily basis; the words slip away after a moment and irresistibly come back to death as the "final point of life."

So that is what the word "death" almost exclusively refers me to: A being was once alive and is no longer. A person did his little stretch on the path of time, wrote his own story in the grand story of humanity, and now the last page has been turned. He or she has "departed this life," as we often hear people saying. I will later speak of that death as terminal death. In the long story that our existence tells, this is the period that comes to close off the last phrase.

The next chapter will be devoted to terminal death. I query myself about it, and I will, first of all, share some of the questions that obsess me. Then I will say a word about terminal death's work of destruction.

As the reader can see, my objective here is limited. But its pursuit should introduce the stakes raised in the following chapter and, it must be hoped, allow a better understanding of the depths at which the work of daily deaths reaches us.

6
Terminal Death

That I haven't broached the question of terminal death until now is not because I wanted to snugly veil its face, denying its ravages and its destructive work. But I hope I have sufficiently shown how death must not be thrust away and imprisoned in this sort of beyond-the-last-moment of our lives. It is to-day, here and now, that we have to pick up the challenge of death, because it's here and now that death and life, together, are beckoning to us.

In dislodging the presence of death all the way into the most banal moments of everyday life we aren't calming for good the anxieties, even the anguish, that can arise in us once we start thinking about terminal death. Isn't each one of us, however, invited to change his or her view of death?

A Few Questions

It will have been easy to guess that I am questioning my-self about terminal death, more specifically about the real

59

relations that each of us has today with his or her own terminal death. Is this what we fear above all? The reflections we have pursued up until now about daily deaths authorize, it seems to me, the questions that I now make bold to share.

1. Many people claim they have less fear of terminal death than of the sufferings that threaten to precede it. To be sure, medicine has made enormous progress in alleviating physical pain. In addition, efforts are made to help people die with dignity and to provide a better companionship to the men and women who are facing that ultimate "expiration date." But, for all that, our fear about the moments that will precede our death won't go away. How great a burden of suffering will I have to endure before death comes to tear me away from life? Will I have the strength to live through these sufferings with dignity? During the time of our lives, isn't that fear of the moments preceding terminal death often worse than our apprehension about the actual moment of death? One finds oneself saying, I might as well die "a sudden death."

2. My father showed his fear of death so openly that we all feared the day when he would come face to face with it. A metastasized cancer carried him off quickly and quite gently. When he fell into unconsciousness during his last hours, we went to get our mother. As soon as she arrived at the foot of his bed, papa suddenly awoke, sat up on his bed, and told her simply,

"How beautiful you look!" And, having made that last declaration of love, he lapsed into unconsciousness again. Then after a few hours he died peacefully. Despite what we can imagine and fear today, how can we know that our meeting with death won't take place just as gently and serenely?

3. The death of a beloved person, of a parent, of a very close friend, inflicts a deep wound on "those left behind." Death leaves me orphaned of someone whose affection taught me the meaning of life and, in a sense, gave birth to my own humanity. I was making my way with a person whose life and love opened me to the mystery of life and love. And now a physical separation comes to break off my relationship with him or her. From now on we'll no longer walk side by side, it will no longer be possible to speak to one another or, still more simply, to be silent together, united as we were by a mutual tenderness. I feel abandoned. I, too, have been visited by death; death wreaks its havoc in me. I have to die to a relationship that had become one of my reasons for living. Hence we can wonder: If we feel so broken by that death, is it mostly for that person and what has happened to him or her? Isn't it rather for ourselves, the "survivors," now forced to come to terms with the tear in the whole fabric of our life today?

4. In the face of terminal death, writes Jean-Paul Sartre, "We would have to compare ourselves to a prisoner on death row, who bravely prepares for his last pun-

ishment, who expends all his efforts to look good on the scaffold, and who in the meantime gets carried off by an epidemic of Spanish flu...."[11] Sartre has been accused, not without reason, of advancing a vision of death that sinks into absurdity and fatalism: Not every death is a sort of road accident that comes unexpectedly and carries us off without warning. Still, there is some truth in what he says here. Nobody has the power to control the moment and the circumstances of the encounter with his or her own terminal death: the countless traffic accidents, the terrorist bombs that kill blindly, the disease that strikes with lightning speed and leaves no time for preparation. When we think of our death, we probably dream of a long approach allowing us to "tame" and pacify it. But it's pointless to prepare myself carefully for death, to get ready to cut a fine figure, to sharpen my courage or try to learn serenity. Who (or what) can assure me that death won't suddenly appear "like a thief in the night"?

5. It's normal for an aged person to be preoccupied by terminal death. The "due date" approaches. On the other hand, how could anyone eliminate it from her thoughts and heart, how not to struggle daily with it, when she knows that she is stricken with a disease that promises a quick end to her days? So, the point is not to deny those lived situations that create a sort of immediate companionship with terminal death. But how are things with the majority of us? At twenty, forty, or sixty years of age, we work, we enjoy ourselves, we

rest, we love. In short, we are alive. So I ask: Does terminal death haunt our daily existence sufficiently so that when we say that life is a grappling with death we mean terminal death?

A Work of Destruction

These questions don't magically eliminate terminal death and the procession of sufferings that can accompany it. On the other hand, no one can live his life without the thought of his own death entering, furtively, into the field of his consciousness. We would prefer to ignore it, to slam the door in its face. But no suit of armor is strong enough to ward off the unexpected visits of that unwanted stranger.

Some people seem not to struggle at all with terminal death as an invincible adversary. On the subject of death, their words are stamped with serenity. Death, they say, is part of life, of their lives. It is the final passage, part and parcel of the innumerable passages that have made up their lives. Others, for very different reasons, long for the coming of death. "If God would only come for me...." They are exhausted from having suffered so much. Their life has been too painful, even cruel. It continues to break them in their body, their spirit, their loves. Their last moment will be—finally!—deliverance.

But perhaps I'm wrong to think that most humans, during the time of their history, aren't on tranquil terms with death. Am I wrong to argue that, far from consider-

ing it a deliverance, we try to put off the day of reckon-
ing as long as possible? Not without reason, some people
avoid thinking about it altogether or do everything to
sweep it out of their consciousness.

The Grim Reaper: That's how painters have often rep-
resented terminal death. It comes with its scythe to reap
through our lives, to reap life itself. Its first labor is to
cut, to tear away, an existence that, in spite of everything,
we continue to cling to.

What are some of the uprootings that we can already
sense in advance and fear? There is the uprooting, though
apparently banal, of the little habits that make up the
fabric of my everyday world, which have colonized the
meager landscape of my life, have made it familiar and
habitable, allowing me to live in it with relative happiness. Death is the uprooting of the pleasures that burst
like bubbles and make some of my days sparkle, the pleasures of a good meal shared in joy, of a catchy tune, of
caresses given or received; the uprooting of a commitment in which I had invested my energies and which will
remain uncompleted, of work, perhaps passionately ex-
citing work, that I will never see accomplished. It is also
the uprooting of happiness and loves and friendships that
come to me like the loveliest of gifts: to love and be loved,
to approach someone, driven by the gusts of tenderness,
to welcome the looks that find me beautiful. It is the uprooting of a relationship of which we have the impression that it lies fallow because a pardon has failed to come
alive and be formulated, or the words have not yet got-

ten around to expressing, or expressing clearly, an affection that, nonetheless, made life live; the uprooting of the "flesh of my flesh," of children that parents have brought into the world and over whom their patience had long and patiently watched. Then, too, death is the uprooting of a love that has known how to translate itself into the long-term, the ever-young fidelity of couples who, whether in sunlight or in storms, and without ever sinking into dreary mechanical habit, were able to reinvent gestures of tenderness (their eyes continue to glow when they look at each other; each one's hands seek out the other's; the two would like this long and beautiful pilgrimage never to end).

And After Death...?

If only we knew what happens after death. Worse yet: If only we knew that anything happens. And here is a second feature of terminal death: It mows down our lives without providing reason with an unshakable guarantee that its work isn't the ultimate absurdity. Is there "someplace" where we will be united with the persons we have loved? Is there something? Someone?

L'Express recently published an interview[12] with Jean Guitton, who is now ninety-three years old. This old convinced Christian, a professional philosopher, the author of more than fifty books, was asked: "When you are asked about eternity, you say: 'I don't know what the beyond is because, precisely, it's the beyond.' Are you afraid of it?"

And Guitton answers: "In the face of death I sense, first of all, a great curiosity, because I'm finally going to find out if what I said about eternity is true or false!" A surprising affirmation on the part of someone who has, in fact, written a very beautiful book about time and eternity. He doesn't know what the beyond is; he's not sure that he spoke the truth about eternity.

At least, many people will think, he's lucky enough to believe that there is a beyond, an eternity. But no one has ever come back from eternity to tell us what it's made of. Still more, no truly human being, of flesh and blood, has come back from death to tell us that there is an eternity. How can we demonstrate and prove that death opens out upon eternity?

But then, too, and by the same token, how can we demonstrate or prove that there is nothing beyond terminal death?[13] Let's be clear on this point: Both the existence of eternity and its nonexistence demand an act of faith, whether that faith be religious or of some other kind. No biological necessity, no reasoning by the intelligence, no mathematical formula, can have the force of proof on this matter.

Death uproots all sorts of happiness, great and small. It thrusts us toward the unknown by concluding the text of our lives with an immense question mark. How could death not cause fear, a fear that can sometimes turn to anguish?

7
The Work of Daily Deaths

For anyone who decides to put into practice the words of Jesus, "doing what is possible" has nothing in common with a lazy, irresponsible sloppiness. On the contrary. The more a human being commits herself to it, the more she must confront death and live through mourning.

It's surprising, but when we talk about mourning, we almost always mean the afflicted state of those who are left behind after the death of someone close to them. But why not talk about the griefs, so many and so often cruel, that have to be gone through by persons who know that they are on the threshold of their own terminal death? And why throw a veil over the griefs that have to be lived out in the daily round of our lives, in the decisions facing every one of us? If those decisions are often hard ones, if sometimes we put them off as long as possible, that's probably because of the grim visage of every decision, because of its burden of death, of the uprootings that it demands and all the mourning to which it invites us.

The thread of reflection leads us to speak of the work of daily deaths in language astonishingly close to that used with reference to terminal death. The latter *uproots* and leads to *where we're not quite sure.* Isn't it the same with the deaths that we have to decide to live out day after day?

So Many Griefs to Live Out

It seems to me that those who freely decide to do everything are exposing themselves to griefs and uprootings of two sorts.

The first kind has become only too clear, one must hope, to need any further emphasis. If I am concerned with inhabiting myself and my world, if I am lucid and tender enough toward myself to live my life by respecting my limits and the limits of the world that is mine, then there are all sorts of theoretically possible choices from which I must uproot myself. The limits of my body, the fragility of my loves, an always imperfect conduct of interpersonal relations, and an equally imperfect organization of collective ties: As a believer I have to grapple, day after day, with many such constraints. No Christian can submit passively to these constraints, because that sort of resignation would be a concrete refusal of the impossible love that faith professes as possible. But neither does anyone have the right to deny the omnipresence of limits and to do any about-face in the presence of the death that every human decision promises. Otherwise, let us say it again, we get the "flight into the sublime."

From the apparently banal decisions that write the story of my existence into the text of every day, down to the long-term life choices, there are so many things that I must give up for lost. So many possibilities that I have to put aside and to which I must die...*so that my decision may live*, so that I may be a living human being.

But here is precisely where the greatest challenge comes in, one that all persons who call themselves Christians must take up: Their faith sends them back to their condition as *human beings*.

It's normal for fear to take hold of us when the greatness of our responsibilities and the gravity of our decisions collide with the smallness of our lives. This fear can even change into anguish. Who am I to honor the responsibilities that have been confided to me? To bear witness to life when sickness marks me with the sign of death? To promise a love that will traverse time when it's hard for me to make even the little gestures of daily tenderness? To educate children in a freedom whose secrets I myself have not yet discovered? To commit myself in the conduct of social, political, and other relations when I have so much trouble living well with myself and with persons close to me?

Fears give birth to the most serious of temptations, the temptation to play at perfection, the temptation to take oneself for God. And thus we are introduced to a second uprooting, to the death that is the hardest to live: We must die to the pretense that we are God.

"Taking oneself for God." The expression keeps returning throughout this book. Do we think that this sort of pretense to perfection will heal our fears and exorcise our anguish? It's a good bet that it will produce the contrary effect, that it will nurture fears instead of calming them.

Here, it seems to me, we meet up again with the analysis by Eugen Drewermann[14]: "Now I understand quite well that people who are targeted by fear, and isolated in their fear, are haunted by the obsession with becoming perfect, after the fashion of a total, absolute being, and ultimately after the fashion of a divine being. They must never commit a single transgression again, never allow themselves a single fault, anything that might be subject to criticism, anything that could be complained about." But this sort of obsession, the German psychotherapist and theologian adds, makes us prisoners of a vicious circle, which "consists in that man *believes he must become like God* to get rid of the fear that it costs him to be human and that, retroactively, *the more he wishes to be God, the more he feels the shame at being no more than human.*"

Faith can be used (hasn't the impossible become possible?) to justify and feed this "obsession with becoming perfect." I discussed this in my last book when I wanted to spell out the nature of *arrogance*, that perverted form of pride.[15] When they give way to "the fear that it costs to be human" and "believe they have to become like God," human beings, according to Drewermann, "fundamentally impose the logic of anguish and finally sink into a world that no longer knows pity, but only judgment, masks, dissimulation, prejudice."

No one can free himself from the confinements of fear and anxiety, tear off his masks, cure himself of lethal dissimulation and prejudice, without deciding to die to his obsession with becoming perfect, like God. No one can learn pride, tenderness, pity, mercy, and deep down, freedom, unless she dies to her appetite for a messianic control over her life and the lives of others. God is God! And it is by a *free gift of engendering* that I can live the pride of a son or a daughter of God.

I will be denied the apprenticeship of that pride if I see myself as, and act like, the alpha and omega of my own existence, father and mother of my life, capable of engendering myself into freedom. So we have to learn that there are no real decisions without *loosening our grip*, without *releasing*, and for a Christian believer, without letting go on behalf of God the engenderer.

The Silences of God

In the concrete world of my daily existence, death comes to uproot. But to fling me toward what? Toward whom? This sort of question introduces us to the second task of death.

God has the art of falling silent precisely at the moments when we have the greatest need for him to speak. He doesn't dictate to me the decision I should make when I find myself exposed, for example, to a particularly delicate moment in our life as a couple or of the education of our children. Or when I'm looking for the solution to social evils, or when we have to make a political choice on which the future of our people depends. Who or what can guarantee me into nothingness, but direct me toward someone who loves me and wants to show me love?

Sometimes God seems so terribly absent when I would like to decide to be alive *in* the deaths that a sick body offers me, *in* my restless questioning about the meaning of life, *in* the wounds of my loves. Who or what can guarantee me, beyond the shadow of a doubt, that I have to let go on behalf of God who is already there and already helping to heal me?

I think that God is silent so that we can take the floor. He *has to* be silent so that our words can be humanly free.[16] I can discover after the fact, sometimes a very long time after my decision, that he was there, lovingly and respectfully present to my freedom. Still, at the moment of decision, what a burden that silence can be to live out!

Let's recall once again the cry of Jesus: "My God, my God, why have you forsaken me?" (Matthew 27:46). At the end of his existence on earth, Jesus runs into the heavy silence of God. The disciples, one after another, have dropped him. And now he feels abandoned not just by the men and women who have followed him up till then, but by the very one to whom he wished to consecrate his entire life. God falls silent. He seems to have forgotten the man who lived only for him.

There, for a believer, is the most terrible of deaths: the death that God's silences make us live through.

Part Four

When Death Comes to Visit Us

8

So That the Dead May Not Kill the Life in Us

*W*e had flung ourselves, eight students and myself, into a long three-month pilgrimage to Jerusalem. At the end of three weeks, I was sure that the group would break up. We were living in campgrounds, everyone constantly together with everyone else, amid the clash of mentalities, genders, and different states of life. An old proverb, which we regularly repeated to ourselves, helped us to hold on: "Only crazy people thought the thing wasn't impossible. And they did it!"

My earlier book was right to argue that faith is not for people who are too wise. You have to be insane to confess the tenderness of the God of Jesus Christ and his infinite respect for human freedom, to affirm his presence at the heart of the decisions that make of us beings who are humanly alive. There is no decision to live that, in fact, isn't also a decision to die. The omnipresence of limits reminds us that we are not God. Ultimately it invites us to make the most serious of decisions, the one to let go. But even in the act of release, God refuses to decide in our place. He is silent. Only madmen, in fact, can believe that life and death are never impossible.

As actors in that great play of life and death, let's not give in to the temptation to affirm too rapidly a definitive victory, in Jesus Christ, of life over death. Until the very end we have to mistrust answers that come too soon: They haven't listened enough to the questions, and they risk accenting the pain of life instead of healing it.

Here I would like to return to the words by Drewermann quoted in the Introduction: "Only those who have the courage to 'descend into hell' can talk about 'heaven' and in that way try to snatch a whole life from the captivity of death." If faith wants to turn itself into hope and bear witness to a life that is stronger than any death, it indeed has to have courage, the courage to unflinchingly get into the deaths we die every day.

The descent into the depths of the abyss, all the way into the silence of God, has already taught us, it seems to me, important things about what it means to live as Christians. In closing, I will content myself to take up a few of them once more. It's not that I want, with a wave of a magic wand, to make the specter of daily deaths vanish. Rather, I hope to extract some conditions that have to be met if we don't want the deaths to kill the life in us, if we want our hope to remain stubborn in its desire to snatch life away from the captivity of death.

Knowing How to Recognize One's Limits

The health of our Christian life demands that first of all we know how to recognize as lucidly as possible the limits that encumber our existence. I know that this isn't always easy. How much time does it take for sick or aging persons to acknowledge the limits that have now been imposed by their bodies, the lessening of choices that remain possible for them and, above all, the activities and commitments they must now renounce? Still, I don't know how, without taking a clear-eyed look at our limits, we can pursue the long apprenticeship of the life of faith.

Have we learned, however, that faith itself demands this sort of acknowledgment of limits?

I had left the hospital on Good Friday, still shaken by a stay that had begun in the intensive care unit. The following Sunday I decided to refresh my hope at the paschal Eucharist of a small community. The homily was fine and reflected a deep faith in the omnipotence of the Resurrection. And yet it struck me as strange and irrelevant. Far from quickening my hope, it created a discomfort that resembled sadness. Why did it produce that effect?

In fact, I felt myself impelled to draw a line separating the Resurrection (or, more accurately, the way that the homily talked about it) from what I had just been through in the hospital. The celebrant was right to invite me to enter into the life of the Risen One. But that entry seemed to demand that I wipe away the previous days, that I impose silence on the suffering I had experienced. A question formulated itself in me: *Must one say nothing about limits and death in order to talk about life in a Christian way?*

Anyone who has suffered a little (does that mean all of us?) will understand, I'm sure, the meaning of the question I have just raised.

I have no intention of denying that faith invites us to let ourselves be swept away by the current of the Resurrection. But to experience to what extent life, in Jesus Christ, is stronger than any death, is it necessary and possible and desirable from a Christian standpoint to act as if our existence was no longer touched by limits? And hence by the deaths that these limits call into life when the time for decision making comes? How can we feel respected and loved, in all that we are and in all that we live, if faith in the Resurrection of Jesus condemns to insignificance our griefs of yesterday and today, as well as those promised for tomorrow?

It's not the limits themselves that strike fear into our hearts. What we worry about, more or less consciously, are the decisions that await us and will make us die to the pretense that we can be everything and do everything. If, moreover, I don't recognize my limits and refuse to maintain a convivial relationship with them, how can I live free, in the manner of a man or woman who is responsible for his or her decisions? Such a lack of tenderness toward oneself, and so toward the limits that I am, leads straight to a paralysis of freedom.

Is there anything more harmful, in fact, than to play the game of perfection? Either I will boast of having, for this or that given situation, the secret of "the" ideal decision, and I will try to force my life and that of others into it. In that case I become a moralizer imposing instead of proposing, someone who judges and condemns all the more easily because he is himself incapable of moving on to action, of putting his ideals into practice, in his own life. Or I will remain indefinitely in suspense, constantly putting off the moment of decision until, ultimately, I become incapable of deciding anything at all. Since there is such a vast distance between the bright perfection to which I lay claim and the chiaroscuro of the situations that life gives me to live through, why and how should I reach any decision? At all events, any decision would be a betrayal of the ideal. Occasionally masking my indecision behind the appearance of a sage who is unwilling to rush anything, I am waiting. During that wait, however, life goes on without my shouldering the responsibilities that it continues to assign me.

Perhaps this lack of respect for limits is meant to save faith or the absolute status of faith. We must repeat: We are baptized into the Resurrection of Jesus Christ, but also into his death. Jesus himself, in his saving work, refused to short-circuit death. All his disciples who intend to be faithful to him and to put his teaching into practice are therefore driven to recognize their own limits, and in that way to die to the imagined perfection of "chemically pure" decisions. Paradoxically, perhaps, this difficult demand of truth has to be honored if we don't want the daily deaths to kill the life in us.

Resisting the Temptation of Shortcuts

Some readers will find me pretentious, but I can't help finding that many forms of so-called Christian spirituality do a bad job of teaching us how to die each day. These spiritualities, if I may be permitted the expression, all too often run to "the soft and sloppy."

Nowadays we hear less and less—and so much the better for that—the exhortations of the *voluntarist* or *dolorist* school that has left so deep a mark on our Catholic mentality: "It's not so bad to suffer, you *do* have to merit heaven...." Lately there's been more lapsing into *consolation*: "You're going through a bad time. But don't worry, there's a light waiting for you at the end of the tunnel." Still more frequently, they claim to awaken hope, when it's really *optimism* that they're calling for: Since we believe in a victory of life over death that is always possible, the "true" Christian, we are given to understand, should be a spontaneous and permanent admirer, possessed by joy, wonderstruck by the song of the little birds or the smile of a child. But Christian hope doesn't depend on the good health of our hormones—or on our psychological energy. It has little to do with facile, victorious flashes of optimism. It is very often poor and weak. Isn't it called, most of the time, to change into a patient, difficult, and stubborn perseverance?

Shortcuts tempt us. In particular, as I have suggested, the shortcut that would allow us to move right now into a "full" life without having to pass through death, without living out death as well.

We have a mad imagination when it comes to inventing ways of avoiding the daily face-to-face confrontation with death, a grappling from which no one knows in advance whether he or she will emerge a winner.

When death visits us, for example, we can always hope for a miracle. But it seems to me profoundly unhealthy, from a Christian point of view, to pin one's life on waiting for a miracle. Or to make others believe that miracles are the standard operating procedure for Christian life.

More generally speaking, we see the emergence in our time of all sorts of approaches and practices that guarantee life, nothing but life, by claiming to magically exorcise death. And I'm always surprised to note how many persons use these shortcuts, even become the apostles of them, all the while calling themselves Christians.

Let me cite a few instances of such shortcuts. I don't mean to laugh at them; for, despite their apparent banality, they probably reveal a suffering that is too heavy to bear, the fear of a death that has to be lived through, perhaps even of anguish.

- Angels, for example, are presently in style. Just recently I came across a book that shows how to get in direct communication with them and to guarantee their protection for oneself. Even if one admits the existence of angels and the long tradition that assigns to them the role of protectors, one may wonder about our supposed power to *control* their intervention and to force them, somehow, to come deliver us from the deaths we are living out or the deaths that await us.

- Prompted by an affection that I don't doubt, a friend of mine built a "spiritual pyramid" (pyramids, too, are in fashion) that envelops my apartment and that will shield me against all malignant powers, especially illness.

- Someone has recently warned me against the black ring that I wear: black, it seems, weakens the antibodies and undermines our health. The simple act of removing the ring would thus be a pledge of better health. On the other hand, another person swears that I'll get beneficial results if I rub the black ring while making a wish for healing.

Since these shortcuts spread so easily, even in circles with a Christian tradition, I wonder about the kinds of spirituality that we have inherited and offer to our world today. Do they really take seriously the daily death that no shortcut allows us to avoid, that we are forced to struggle with? There is an abrupt quality in death, a cutting, a rupture that the heart and reason find intolerable. For my part, I don't see how Christian faith would ever promise and permit us to escape, as if by magic, from the sufferings and the lacerations caused by death lived out on a daily basis.

Allowing Oneself to Doubt

A lawyer in his sixties was telling me that he had lost his faith one day back, when he became a young adult and started to doubt the answers given to his questions. My first reaction was one of incomprehension, but also of pain. How could people have talked to him about the Christian faith so that he thought of doubt as the contrary of faith? How did he get to the point of assuming that the arrival of doubts necessarily resulted in a "loss of faith"? Then I recalled the first years *I* had spent studying theology, and how reticent we always were with our professors: "Your answer is logical," we often felt. "It's part of a solid and coherent system of thought. The only problem is, this system and your answer don't seem to have understood our question."

Am I wrong to suggest that we have been taught too much to think of faith in the form of answers? That means ready-made answers, worked out in advance, answers spelled out even before hearing the questions that we ask ourselves about the meaning of life. Thus we had in hand a sort of catechism of the perfect little Christian in which even the existence of God was logically demonstrated and proved. I also recall our manual of moral theology, two hefty volumes that prepared us to answer correctly all the "cases" that might be presented to the confessor. I have the impression that I'm caricaturing as I write. But it's true, it was in this universe of answers that we learned, it seems to me, to think about faith, to live it and offer it to others.

In this perspective, doubt was obviously unjustified and unjustifiable. Because the space of doubt opens up only when faith refuses to be a passive acceptance of answers that have been predefined and formulated once and for all. The space of doubt opens up only when believers allow themselves to live out their faith in the form of a question.

The God of Jesus Christ doesn't want to impose himself on, or to substitute himself for, our human freedom. He proposes to live out his own tenderness in the hollow core of the decisions—never totally clear or perfectly free—that are our responsibility. Who can guarantee me, positively "beyond any doubt," that my decision constitutes *the* right decision, the one that corresponds perfectly to the inspirations of God's tenderness? Besides, God chooses to be silent at the very moment when I live out a grappling with death; and this silence, for a believer, is the most painful of deaths. Is God really offering us in Jesus Christ a life capable of victory over death?

If the God of Jesus Christ is like that, doubt is far from being contrary to faith, or a sin against faith. God himself, through the infinite discretion of his love, authorizes doubt....

It is already profoundly liberating for Christian believers to acknowledge and make their own this judiciousness of their God—*and in that way to allow themselves the possibility of doubting.* Doubts are already hard enough to live through when they arise at the same time as a rendezvous with death. These difficulties shouldn't be made worse by adding on pathological guilt, the sickness suffered by anyone who doesn't even give himself or herself the permission to doubt.

"Faith," said Georges Bernanos, "is twenty-four hours of doubt minus two minutes of hope."

Declaring Oneself a Survivor

Certain moments can be truly painful: Everyone has known days when hope seemed very close to desperation. These are days with the taste of death, crushed beneath the clouds that no ray of light manages to pierce. Remembering sunny days, one tells oneself that life could become beautiful again, but one says this the way one affirms an abstract principle. There is no spontaneous outpouring here. The taste of life has been quenched. One spends days, sometimes weeks and months, without any sense that as life is passing it is energizing the days and the months. If God maintains a place in our field of consciousness, his presence is perceived as the presence of someone who isn't there. One doesn't live, one tries to survive.

Why should we be ashamed at such times of declaring ourselves survivors? There is nothing shameful here and, for believers, nothing contrary to faith. It could even be dangerous to play the game of good health, to make ourselves believe that things are at their best and to stubbornly insist on projecting this image to others. Relations with oneself and with other people would be falsified by this approach. They would turn into a lie, and lies never make good servants of life.

Declaring oneself a survivor means, first of all, *consenting to the impoverishments of the present.* Alcoholics Anonymous works miracles with a disarmingly simple principle: "Twenty-four hours at a time." If deaths that are more trying than usual make any one day seem too long to live through, take it one hour at a time!

To be sure, the point here is not to let oneself glide down the slope of an irresponsible complacency. Later I'll return to the necessity, even in these trying moments, of always deciding, of at least trying to decide something. But we would be locking ourselves up in desperation by imposing on ourselves all-too-demanding responsibilities that would only worsen the sense of powerlessness that we find ourselves bogged down in today.

Declaring oneself a survivor can also mean *carrying out a work of memory* that will be able to nurture the present or at least help us to bear it. We have believed that even the impossible is possible; we have had experiences strengthening that faith. It is important to commemorate it, but we mustn't abandon ourselves to nostalgia by imprisoning ourselves in memories that have accumulated over the course of the years. Nostalgia is a bad guide to life and badly serves the opening of the present. The task of memory is rather to rediscover, as if beneath our recollections, the thread of a certain fidelity.

Do we have the feeling that this fidelity no longer exists? Perhaps, thanks to the obstinate work of memory, it will announce its presence once again by bringing new projects to birth.

After having cried out to God his feeling of abandonment, Jesus sent up a last murmur, a murmur louder than all the cries in the world: "Father, into your hands I commend my spirit" (Luke 23:46). The fidelity of an entire life is recalled and summed up in that murmur. Through his work of memory, Jesus has just consecrated the new name of God by revealing, all the way to the extreme limit of his life, that God is a Father, that is, a God whose only desire is to engender humans to life. The whole course of time to follow would be transformed by this....

Declaring oneself a survivor, finally, means agreeing *to define oneself* differently with regard to the future. The more one lives through the crushing limits and the trials of mourning, the more one is inclined to make radical decisions. For some even suicide may seem attractive— less unbearable, at any rate, than the pain of living in which they find themselves snared. Is it really time, however, to come to grips in an irremediable fashion with the middle and long term of our lives?

It may be that the moment is favorable for a radical challenge and the stimulus to desire a new life. Persons alienated in their dependence on alcohol or drugs, to take only one example, often realize, at the lowest depth of their pain, that no other way out is possible except a total break with the past and the creation of completely different habits for the future. But nothing will achieve by magic and forever the transformation they so ardently dream of. Ineluctably, such persons, like everyone for whom a death will bring survival, see the reaffirmation of the necessity of "twenty-four hours at a time."

So this is the time for patience. We must learn the patience of time…patience toward other people, and especially toward ourselves and the life that is slowly resurfacing in us. We have to tell ourselves that if the deaths are not to kill the life in us, our patience will always be a very pale reflection of the tender patience that the God of Jesus Christ feels for us.

Welcoming the Life and Love of Others

Anyone who is plunged "into the depths of the abyss" no longer quite knows how to manage his or her relations with others. During the first stages of a serious encounter with death, when the grief is stifling, our reflex response may be to isolate ourselves, to fall back upon our sufferings, since they are lived with intensity and seem to be incommunicable. Besides, who could understand what we ourselves don't understand? Relations are scarcely easier in the moments when a certain communication has once more become possible. We are heading up a mountain crest that is hard to negotiate. How not to alienate others with the incessant tale of our troubles? How, on the other hand, to be truthful with ourselves and with them if we force ourselves to say nothing about the experience—even though it is a crucial one—that we are living through? We have lost our habitual orientation, we don't quite know how to approach others or how to welcome them.

Still, we guess that there can be no salvation without seclusion. And what we surmise in this way constitutes an appeal by life. It's important to answer that appeal. Even if we don't have a good sense of how communication with others could prevent the deaths from killing the life in us, it's necessary to *put our trust* in others.

Of its own accord Christian faith invites us to have this sort of trust. I have mentioned the important work of memory. What we must particularly keep in mind here is the place of others in our lives: *They are a sacrament of the God of Jesus Christ and have a mission of revealing to us the innumerable aspects of his face.*[17]

God, we think, has absented himself from our lives. He has fallen silent. But what if he was silent the better to allow others to speak, and to speak to us? And, who knows, to tell us how life is already bringing our deaths back to life?

Experience teaches us that every decision profits from communication with others. In those decisions we also get the chance (or is it the grace?) to find less insane the deaths that these decisions promise. Hence the necessity of a true sharing community where life and the daily deaths of each one of us can be welcomed by everyone, welcomed in truth and tenderness, in the truth *of* tenderness. The delicate problem of educating children, the complex laws of love, whether so-and-so should marry or be single, duty and the demands of justice—everything gains by being shared.

The answers will probably be few and far between, since in the final analysis everyone is responsible for his or her own decisions. But is there anything more liberating than to be able, at least, to share one's questions? And to discover how life, from the very inner depths of those questions, inches its way along? We are surprised and end up learning that the questions, often more than the answers, open up the thickness of the present and uncover the future that no one ever suspected.

It becomes even more imperative to put our trust in others, in their capacity to listen to and lovingly welcome us, when death seems invincible, when our griefs are so heavy that we have a hard time seeing how they won't kill life. That kind of trust is not self-evident. We can at least try, in our poverty, one small step in the direction of others.

Those others will not be very numerous. They will even be rare, given that the questions to be shared rise up from the lowest depths within us and head off to encounter, in others, the most secret part of their existence. Even if they don't have the answers, even if they don't understand our questions, that powerlessness doesn't stifle their capacity to welcome: a sort of loving empathy that comes into play well beyond or short of answers and questions.

It may even happen that we are incapable, at certain

moments, of telling the persons closest to us about the death we are living through. Is it necessary, then, or even desirable, to want to "explain," whatever the cost? We can do nothing but abandon ourselves to the tenderness of others. We can only welcome the beauty of the look they bestow on us, let ourselves be carried by them with the unbearable burden that we are living through. We can drink to their life, to their gusto for living, as at a wellspring; we can go weep in the arms that they open to us....

When one is a survivor, trust ought not to be ashamed or afraid of becoming abandonment to the love of others.

And Continuing to Decide...

"Father, into your hands I commend my spirit." We might understand that last word of Jesus on the cross as an act of resignation. He has just undergone atrocious sufferings, which have drained his blood and his energies. He finds himself terribly alone, he who has lived and preached only one law, the law of love: "I give you a new commandment, that you love one another" (John 13:34). He has struggled all his life against the powers that disfigure both the face of God and the face of humans; and now these powers seem to be emerging victoriously from the struggle: They are stronger. He had come so that humans "[might] have life, and have it abundantly" (John. 10:10); and now he himself is visited by death. In giving up his spirit into the hands of God, what is Jesus doing but signing the affidavit of a failure, the failure of an entire life? Let's repeat Jesus' other word, which prevents us from understanding the last one as a resignation: "For this reason the Father loves me, because I lay down my life, in order to take it up again. No one takes it from me, but I lay it down of my own accord" (John 10:17–18). Neither the weary labors of life, nor the sufferings of the Passion, nor the apparent failure of his plan; neither the religious or political powers, nor God—no one and nothing forces him to part with his life. In the end, what might seem to be an admission of defeat becomes, rather, the expression of an ultimate decision and hence the most revelatory act of Jesus' freedom.

When Christian women and men, facing daily death, commemorate Jesus and his life as a free man, they inevitably remind themselves of the responsibility of their faith: Even when they are visited by death, God still wants to depend on their decisions. In truth, and especially when the daily deaths try to crush us in the depths of the abyss, we learn that "faith is a *decision*. Believing means deciding to believe, deciding to continue to believe."[18]

Deciding! We should always decide something, even if in the eyes of other people or in my own my decision will be of little consequence and seems insignificant. I should always raise this question: Given the limits that I am living through and the grief into which they plunge me, what can I do today that would be an affirmation of life? What can I decide today that would anchor me in fidelity to myself and to practicing Jesus' words?

The face of the world and the course of history will perhaps not be transformed by what I decide to do. But who knows if I might not succeed in opening a breach in death, in my death, a breach that will deliver me from my grave by liberating the current of life?

Sometimes death can be so invasive, and the abyss so deep, that we can't do anything at all. It's no good trying to free up the horizon of possibilities; no action can be decided on. If we stubbornly insist on believing that Jesus wants to be anchored in our decisions, then this faith manages only to make more insupportable the terrible silence of life—up till the moment when, with no answer coming, we discover that perhaps we have to change the question. Instead of asking ourselves exclusively what we can *do*, instead of searching for activities to engage in, we wonder: Couldn't I decide to *be* differently?

This shift is extremely important. It's enough to re-open the horizon by opening a new passage to life. Perhaps it's not possible for me to do very much. But I can decide to *be* differently in the face of life, in the face of others, even if only by changing my view of myself, of others, and of life. I could learn, for example, to be more available, to give a warmer welcome, to have compassion for the sufferings of others, to marvel at all the victories of life....

In the moments of heavy deaths, we might envy those who are marching gaily toward a future that nothing seems to block. We can be jealous of their victorious dynamism and of the scope of their plans. But nothing is more precious than the victories scored over the daily round of life by people who are survivors. Nothing is more precious than the slight opening that succeeds in sweeping along their today in the direction of tomorrow. Their freedom in action has become hope in action, and that hope has already snatched away a whole life from the captivity of death.

Notes

1. Eugen Drewermann, *La Barque du soleil: La mort et la résurrection en Égypte ancienne et dans l'Évangile* (Paris: Seuil, 1994), p. 14.
2. *Foi chrétienne et fierté humaine* (Montreal/Paris: Paulines, Éditions de l'Atelier, 1966).
3. *L'Actualité religieuse*, 140 (January 15, 1996), 31.
4. Cf. *Foi chrétienne*, pp. 34ff.
5. Cf. Ibid., especially pp. 46–51 and 89-93.
6. Cf. Ibid., especially pp. 43-51.
7. *Le Point critique*, Paris, DDBB (1970), 130.
8. Cf. *Foi chrétienne*, pp. 86ff.
9. Hans Urs Von Balthasar, *L'amour seul est digne de foi* (Paris: Aubier, 1966), p. 78.
10. Cf. p. 10.
11. *L'Être et le néant* (Paris, 1943), p. 617.
12. N. 2275 (February 16, 1995).
13. In the interview cited above (cf. p. 24) the philosopher A. Comte-Sponville, a declared atheist, is right to affirm: "The point is to believe that God doesn't

exist, not to know it. Anyone who would say: '*I know that God doesn't exist*' is not an atheist, he's an imbecile. The truth is that we don't know. And because we don't know, it all comes down to believing or not believing." The philosopher is careful to add: "By the way, I would say the same thing for believers. If somebody tells me: '*I know that God exists,*' for me he's not a believer, he's an imbecile."

14. *La parole qui guérit* (Paris: Cerf, 1993). The quotations are taken from pages 44–45, and the italics are mine.

15. Cf. *Foi chrétienne*, pp. 41 ff.

16. I'll be developing this theme further in my next book.

17. Cf. *Foi chrétienne*, pp. 44–78.

18. J.C. Sagne, "Du besoin à la demande, ou la conversion du désir dans la prière," *Pax*, 167 (June 1973), 11.